Indexes

A CHAPTER FROM
THE CHICAGO
MANUAL OF STYLE

EIGHTEENTH
EDITION

The University of Chicago Press
Chicago and London

The University of Chicago Press, Chicago 60637
The University of Chicago Press, Ltd., London
© 2024 by The University of Chicago
Published 2024
Printed and bound by CPI Group (UK) Ltd, Croydon, CR0 4YY

33 32 31 30 29 28 27 26 25 24   1 2 3 4 5

ISBN-13: 978-0-226-83768-0 (paper)
ISBN-13: 978-0-226-83769-7 (ebook)
DOI: https://doi.org/10.7208/chicago/9780226837697.001.0001

♾ This paper meets the requirements of ANSI/NISO Z39.48-1992
(Permanence of Paper).

The Chicago Manual of Style is a registered trademark of
The University of Chicago.

15 **Indexes**

OVERVIEW

15.1   **The back-of-the-book index as model.** This chapter offers basic guidelines for preparing and editing an alphabetically arranged index that will appear at the end of a book-length work. Though the advice is modeled primarily on the requirements of a book with fixed page numbers (as in print or PDF) or other fixed locators (like the paragraph numbers in this manual), the principles should apply also to works that lack such mileposts (see 15.13). General principles of indexing are covered, as are the specifics of Chicago's preferred style in matters of typography, alphabetizing, and the like.

15.2   **Why index?** In this age of searchable text, the need for an index made with human input is sometimes questioned. But a good index can do what a plain search cannot: It gathers all the substantive terms and subjects of the work, sorts them alphabetically, provides cross-references to and from related terms, and includes specific page numbers or other locators or, for electronic formats, direct links to the text. This painstaking intellectual labor serves readers of any longer work, whether it is searchable or not. For searchable texts, an index provides insurance against fruitless queries and unintended results. For example, if the text reads, "In the 1960s, countries outside the sphere of US and Soviet influence played those two nations against each other," there should be an index entry for "Cold War." A search for that term may not pick this up. In a word, a good index makes the text more accessible.

15.3   **Who should index a work?** The ideal indexer sees the work as a whole, understands the emphasis of the various parts and their relation to the whole, and knows—or guesses—what readers of the particular work are likely to look for and what headings they will think of. The indexer should be widely read, scrupulous in handling detail, analytically minded, well acquainted with publishing practices, and capable of meeting almost impossible deadlines. Although authors know better than anyone else their subject matter and the audience to whom the work is addressed, not all can look at their work through the eyes of a potential reader. Nor do many authors have the technical skills, let alone the time, necessary to prepare a good index that meets the publisher's deadline. Some authors produce excellent indexes. Others would do better to enlist the aid of a professional indexer.

15.4   **The indexer and deadlines.** Most book indexes must be made between the time page proofs are issued and the time they are returned to the typesetter—usually from two to six weeks. (For an illustration of how indexing fits into the overall publishing process for books, see 2.2.) Authors preparing their own indexes will have to proofread as well as index the work in that short time span. Good indexing requires reflection; the indexer needs to stop frequently and decide whether the right choices have been made. A professional indexer, familiar with the publisher's requirements and equipped with specialized software and experience, may be better equipped for such reflection. For those few journals that still publish a volume index (see 1.119), the indexer may have several months to prepare a preliminary index, adding entries as new issues of the journal arrive. The final issue in the volume is typically indexed from page proofs, however, and the indexer may have as little as a week to work on the last issue and prepare the final draft of the index. In a similar manner, page proofs for textbooks and other very large works may arrive in sections over several months, and the index is usually due one to two weeks after the final proofs arrive.

15.5　**The role of software in indexing.** A concordance—or a complete list of terms (typically minus articles, prepositions, and other irrelevant elements) and their page locations or frequency of use—can be produced automatically. But a concordance is not the same as an index. Most indexes of the type described in this chapter are produced from scratch, typically from paginated page proofs, either electronic or hard copy, generated by a page-layout program. Word processors are typically used in entering and editing terms and locators in a separate document and can provide rudimentary help in the process of sorting entries and managing cross-references. Most professional indexers use dedicated indexing software, which provides shortcuts for creating and editing entries and automates formatting, allowing the indexer to focus on the creative analysis of the text. This type of software is an essential investment for a professional indexer and may be worth it for an author planning to index many books over time (see 15.113). See also 15.7, 15.13.

15.6　**Single versus multiple indexes.** A single, comprehensive index—one that includes concepts and names of persons and other subjects—is recommended for most works. Certain publications, however, such as lengthy scientific works that cite numerous authors of other studies, may include an index of named authors (see 15.38) in addition to a subject index. An anthology may include an author-and-title index, and a collection of poetry or hymns may have an index of first lines as well as an index of titles. It is generally an advantage if two or more indexes appearing in one work are visually distinct from one another so that users

3

know immediately where they are. In a biological work, for example, the headings in the index of names will all be in roman type and will begin with capital letters, and there will be no subentries, whereas most of the headings in the general subject index will begin lowercase and many subentries will appear; and if there is a taxonomic index, many headings will be in italics. Separate running heads should be used, indicating the title of each index (e.g., Index of Names, Index of Subjects).

15.7 **Embedded indexes.** An embedded index consists of key terms anchored with underlying codes to particular points in the text of an electronic publication. These terms can facilitate a reader's queries to a search engine in much the same way that a good subject index gathers keywords under subject headings to increase the chances that a reader will be led only to the relevant areas of a text. For example, a search for the word "because" in a properly coded online encyclopedia might lead to those passages that discuss the Beatles' *Abbey Road* song "Because" rather than to every instance of the omnipresent conjunction. The principles of selection for embedded indexes are similar to those for traditional back-of-the-book indexes. Many journal publishers, especially in the sciences, rely on standard keyword vocabularies and have largely done away with traditional indexes. On the other hand, many book publishers anchor their back-of-the-book index entries to the electronic files that drive publication in print and other formats in order to facilitate hyperlinked indexes for ebook formats (see also 15.13).

15.8 **Resources for indexers.** For greatly expanded coverage of the present guidelines, along with alternative methods, consult the second edition of Nancy Mulvany's *Indexing Books* (bibliog. 2.5). Anyone likely to prepare a number of indexes should acquire that work. For further reference, see Hans H. Wellisch, *Indexing from A to Z*, and Linda K. Fetters, *Handbook of Indexing Techniques* (bibliog. 2.5).

COMPONENTS OF AN INDEX

Main Headings, Subentries, and Locators

15.9 **Main headings for index entries.** The main heading of an index entry is normally a noun or noun phrase—the name of a person, a place, an object, or an abstraction. In general, count nouns and count noun phrases should be plural rather than singular. An adjective alone should almost never constitute a heading; it should rather be paired with a noun to form a noun phrase. A noun phrase is sometimes inverted to allow the keyword—the word a reader is most likely to look under—to appear first. The heading is typically followed by page (or paragraph) numbers (see 15.12) and sometimes a cross-reference (see 15.15–23). For capitalization, see 15.11.

agricultural collectivization, 143–46, 198

Aron, Raymond, 312–14

Bloomsbury group, 269

Brest-Litovsk, Treaty of, 61, 76, 85

Cold War, 396–437

Communist Party (American), 425

Communist Party (British), 268

imperialism, American, 393, 403

police, Soviet secret. *See* Soviet secret police

prisoners of war, 93

war communism, 90, 95, 125

World War I, 34–61

Yalta conference, 348, 398

15.10 **Index subentries.** An entry that requires more than five or six locators (page or paragraph numbers) is usually broken up into subentries to spare readers unnecessary excursions. A subentry, like an entry, consists of a heading (usually referred to as a subheading), page references, and, rarely, cross-references. Subheadings often form a grammatical relationship with the main heading, whereby heading and subheading combine into a single phrase, as in the first example below. Other subheadings form divisions or units within the larger category of the heading, as in the second example. Both kinds can be used within one index. See also 15.126. For sub-subentries, see 15.27, 15.28.

capitalism: and American pro-Sovietism, 273, 274; bourgeoisie as symbol of, 4, 13; as creation of society, 7; Khrushchev on burying, 480; student protests against, 491, 493

Native American peoples: Chichimec, 67–68; Huastec, 154; Olmec, 140–41; Toltec, 128–36; Zapotec, 168–72

15.11 **Initial lowercase letters in main headings and subheadings.** The first word of a main heading is normally capitalized only if capitalized in text—a proper noun (as in the second example in 15.10), a genus name, the title of a work, and so on. Traditionally, all main headings in an index were capitalized. Chicago recommends this practice only where the subentries are so numerous that capitalized main headings make for easier navigation. Indexes in the sciences, however, should generally avoid initial capitals because the distinction between capitalized and lowercased terms in the text may be crucial. Subheadings are always lowercased unless the keyword is capitalized in text (like "Khrushchev" in the first example in 15.10 and all the subentries in the second example).

15.12 **Locators in indexes.** In a printed work or PDF, locators are usually page numbers, though they can also be paragraph numbers (as in this manual), section numbers, or the like. When discussion of a subject continues for more than a page, paragraph, or section, the first and last numbers (inclusive numbers) are given: 34–36 (if pages), 10.36–41 (if paragraphs), and so on (see 15.14). The abbreviations *ff.* and *et seq.* should never be used in an index. Scattered references to a subject over several pages or sections are usually indicated by separate locators (34, 35, 36; *or* 8.18, 8.20, 8.21). Though the term *passim* has often been used to indicate scattered references over a number of not necessarily sequential pages or sections (e.g., 78–88 passim), individual locators are preferred. For use of the en dash, see 6.83.

15.13 **Indexes for ebooks and other electronic formats.** At a minimum, indexes destined for ebook formats should be linked to the text. Page number data for a printed format can provide the basis of such links, and publishers are encouraged to include this data in their electronic publication formats. In formats with reflowable text, however, the actual place in the text may be several screens beyond the location of the first "page." For this reason, index entries are best linked directly to the passage of text to which they refer. (In works like this manual, links can be made directly to numbered paragraphs.) This approach, though it requires considerable intervention on the part of the publisher or indexer, produces a better experience for the reader. A detailed specification for ebook indexes is available from the World Wide Web Consortium, which maintains the EPUB standard.

15.14 **Inclusive numbers in indexes.** Publishers vary in their preferences for the form of inclusive numbers (also known as continuing numbers). Although the simplest and most foolproof system is to give the full form of numbers everywhere (e.g., 234–235), Chicago prefers its traditional system (presented below), which is efficient and unambiguous. The system is followed in all examples in this chapter. Whichever form is used in the text should be used in the index as well.

First number	Second number	Examples
Less than 100	Use all digits	3–10
		71–72
		96–117

100 or multiples of 100	Use all digits	100–104
		1100–1113
101 through 109,	Use changed part only	101–8
201 through 209, etc.		808–33
		1103–4
110 through 199,	Use two digits unless more	321–28
210 through 299, etc.	are needed to include all	498–532
	changed parts	1087–89
		1496–500
		11564–615
		12991–3001

Roman numerals are always given in full—for example, xxv–xxviii, cvi–cix. In an index that refers to section numbers, the same principles apply as for page numbers (e.g., 16.9–14, 16.141–45). For use of the en dash between numerals, see 6.83; see also 9.62.

Cross-References

15.15   **Cross-references in indexes — general principles.** Cross-references are of two main kinds—*see* references and *see also* references. Each is treated differently according to whether it refers to a main heading or to a subheading. *See* and *see also* are set in italics (but see 15.22). In electronic publication formats, cross-references should link to the terms in the index to which they refer. Cross-references should be used with discretion; an overabundance, besides irritating the reader, may signal the need for consolidation of entries.

15.16   **"See" references and "double posting."** *See* references are used to direct readers from a term they initially looked up to the place in the index where the information they are seeking appears. They should never include locators. *See* references direct a reader from, for example, an informal term to a technical one, a pseudonym to a real name, an inverted term to a noninverted one. They are also used for variant spellings, synonyms, aliases, abbreviations, and so on. The choice of the term under which the full entry appears depends largely on where readers are most likely to look. *See* references should therefore be given only where the indexer believes many readers might otherwise miss the full entry. Further, the indexer and anyone editing an index must make certain that no *see* reference merely leads to another *see* reference. If, on the other hand, the entry to which the *see* reference refers is about the same length as the *see* reference itself, it is often more useful to omit the *see* reference and simply give the page numbers under both headings. Such duplication (or "double posting") will save readers a trip.

> FBI (Federal Bureau of Investigation),
>   145–48
> Federal Bureau of Investigation,
>   145–48
> *rather than*
> Federal Bureau of Investigation. *See*
>   FBI

See also 15.54.

15.17 **"See" references following a main heading.** When a *see* reference follows a main heading, as it usually does, it is preceded by a period and *See* is capitalized. If two or more *see* references are needed, they are arranged in alphabetical order and separated by semicolons. They reflect the capitalization and word order of the main heading.

> adolescence. *See* teenagers; youth
> American Communist Party. *See*
>   Communist Party (American)
> baking soda. *See* sodium bicarbonate
> Clemens, Samuel. *See* Twain, Mark
> Den Haag ('s Gravenhage). *See* Hague,
>   The
> Lunt, Mrs. Alfred. *See* Fontanne, Lynn
> Mormons. *See* Latter-day Saints,
>   Church of Jesus Christ of
> Roman Catholic Church. *See* Catholicism
> The Hague. *See* Hague, The
> Turwyn. *See* Terouenne
> universities. *See* Harvard University;
>   Princeton University; University of
>   Chicago
> Virgin Queen. *See* Elizabeth I
> von Humboldt, Alexander. *See* Humboldt, Alexander von

15.18 **"See" references following a subheading.** When a *see* reference follows a subheading, it is put in parentheses and *see* is lowercased.

> statistical material, 16, 17, 89; as on-
>   line supplement (*see* supplements,
>   online); proofreading, 183

This usage applies to both run-in and indented indexes, and to sub-subentries. See 15.27, 15.28.

15.19 **"See" references to a subheading.** Most *see* references are to a main entry, as in the examples in 15.17. When a cross-reference directs readers to a subentry under another main heading, *see under* may be used.

> lace making. *See under* Bruges
> *Pride and Prejudice*. *See under* Austen,
> Jane

An alternative, to be used when a *see under* reference might fail to direct readers to the right spot, is to drop the word *under* and add the wording of the subheading, following a colon. (Although a comma is sometimes used, a colon is preferred.) The wording of the cross-reference must correspond to that of the relevant subheading so that readers can find it quickly.

> lace making. *See* Bruges: lace making
> *Pride and Prejudice*. *See* Austen, Jane:
> *Pride and Prejudice*

15.20 **"See also" references.** *See also* references direct readers to additional information elsewhere in the index, including related but nonsynonymous concepts. They can be used as an alternative to making the structure of an index more complex. *See also* references are placed at the end of an entry when *additional* information can be found in another entry. When planning *see also* references between related concepts, indexers should make sure the concepts are not actually synonyms that should be combined into one entry. Nor should a *see also* entry lead to an entry that does not list any page numbers not already included in the original entry. (*See also* entries are not the place to show relationships between terms.) In run-in indexes, they follow a period; in indented indexes, they appear on a separate line (see 15.26). *See* is capitalized, and both words are in italics. If the cross-reference is to a subentry under another main heading, the words *see also under* may be used. If two or more *see also* references are needed, they are arranged in alphabetical order and separated by semicolons. As with *see* references, *see also* references must never lead to a *see* reference.

> copyright, 95–100. *See also* permis-
> sion to reprint; source notes
> Maya: art of, 236–43; cities of, 178;
> present day, 267. *See also under*
> Yucatán

If *see also under* does not work in a particular context—for example, when one of the *see also* references is to a main entry and another to a subentry—the word *under* should be dropped and the wording of the subentry added after a colon.

> Maya: art of, 236–43; cities of, 178.
> *See also* Mexican art; Yucatán:
> Maya

When a *see also* reference comes at the end of a subentry—a rare occurrence, and somewhat distracting—it is put in parentheses and *see* is lowercased.

> equality: as bourgeois ideal, 5–6,
> 7; contractual quality, 13; in
> democracy's definition, 24 (*see also*
> democracy); League of the Rights
> of Man debate on, 234–35

15.21 **Correspondence between cross-references and headings.** All cross-referenced headings (and subheadings, if used) should generally be cited in full, with capitalization, inversion, and punctuation exactly as in the heading referred to. But a long heading may occasionally be shortened if no confusion results. For example, in an index with frequent references to Beethoven, "*See also* Beethoven, Ludwig van" could be shortened to "*See also* Beethoven" if done consistently.

15.22 **Italics for "see," "see also," and so forth.** The words *see*, *see under*, and *see also* are normally italicized. But if what follows (e.g., a book title or a word in another language) is in italics, the words are preferably set in roman to distinguish them from the rest of the cross-reference. This is not necessary when they follow italics.

> Austen, Jane. See *Pride and Prejudice*
> *but*
> *Pride and Prejudice.* See Austen, Jane

15.23 **Generic cross-references.** Both *see* and *see also* references may include generic references; that is, they may refer to a type of heading rather than to several specific headings. The entire cross-reference is then set in italics.

public buildings. *See names of individ-*
ual buildings
sacred writings, 345–46, 390–401,
455–65. *See also specific titles*

When generic cross-references accompany specific cross-references,
the former are placed last, even if out of alphabetical order. The conjunction *and* is normally used, following a semicolon (even if the generic cross-reference follows only one other cross-reference).

dogs, 35–42. *See also* American Ken-
nel Club; shelters; *and individual*
breed names

Run-In Versus Indented Indexes

15.24   **Flush-and-hang formatting for indexes.** Indexes are generally formatted
in flush-and-hang (or hanging-indent) style. The first line of each entry,
the main heading, is set flush left, and any following lines are indented.
When there are subentries, a choice must be made between run-in and
indented styles (see 15.25, 15.26). In print publications (and electronic
works modeled on the printed page), indexes are usually set in multiple
columns. In manuscripts, however, columns should not be used (see
15.130).

15.25   **Run-in style for indexes.** In run-in style, the subentries follow the main
entry and one another without starting a new line. They are separated
by semicolons. If the main heading is immediately followed by subentries, it is separated from them by a colon (see first example below). If
it is immediately followed by locators, these are preceded by a comma
and followed by a semicolon (see second example). Further examples
of run-in entries may be seen in 15.10, 15.20, 15.140.

coordinate systems: Cartesian, 14;
distance within, 154–55; time dilation and, 108–14. *See also* inertial
systems; moving systems

Sabba da Castiglione, Monsignor, 209,
337; on cosmetics, 190; on whether
to marry, 210–11; on wives' proper
behavior, 230–40, 350

Chicago and many other publishers generally prefer run-in style because it requires less space. It works best, however, when there is only

one level of subentry (but see 15.27). For the examples above in indented style, see 15.26.

15.26 **Indented style for indexes.** In indented style (also known as stacked style), each subentry begins a new line and is indented (usually one em). No colon appears before the first subheading, and subentries are not separated by semicolons. Runover lines must therefore be further indented (usually two ems) to distinguish them clearly from subentries; whether runover lines belong to the main entry or to subentries, their indentation should be the same. (Indentation is always measured from the left margin, not from the first word in the line above.) *See also* cross-references belonging to the entry as a whole appear at the end of the list of subentries (as shown in the first example below). A *see* or *see also* reference belonging to a specific subentry is placed in parentheses at the end of the subentry, as in run-in indexes (see 15.18, 15.20). See also 15.23.

coordinate systems
  Cartesian, 14
  distance within, 154–55
  time dilation and, 108–14
  See also inertial systems; moving
    systems

Sabba da Castiglione, Monsignor,
  209, 337
  on cosmetics, 190
  on whether to marry, 210–11
  on wives' proper behavior, 230–40,
    350

Indented style is usually preferred in scientific works and reference works (such as this manual). It is particularly useful where subsubentries are required (see 15.28).

15.27 **Sub-subentries in run-in indexes.** If more than a handful of subsubentries are needed in an index, the indented format rather than the run-in type should be chosen. A very few, however, can be accommodated in a run-in index or, better, avoided by repeating a keyword (see example A below). If repetition will not work, subentries requiring subsubentries can be indented, each starting a new line but preceded by an em dash flush with the margin; the sub-subentries are then run in (see example B). Em dashes are *not* used where only one level of subentry is needed.

Example A (run-in index: sub-subentries avoided)

Inuit: language, 18; pottery, 432–37;
  tradition of, in Alaska, 123; tradition of, in California, 127

Example B (run-in index: subentries requiring sub-subentries indented with em dash, sub-subentries run in)

Argos: cremation at, 302; and Danaos of Egypt, 108; Middle Helladic, 77; shaft graves at, 84

Arkadia, 4; Early Helladic, 26, 40; Mycenaean, 269, 306

armor and weapons

— attack weapons (general): Early Helladic and Cycladic, 33; Mycenaean, 225, 255, 258–60; from shaft graves, 89, 98–100; from tholos tombs, 128, 131, 133

— body armor: cuirass, 135–36, 147, 152, 244, 258, 260, 311; greaves, 135, 179, 260; helmets, 101, 135

— bow and arrow, 14, 99, 101, 166, 276

Asine: Early Helladic, 29, 36; Middle Helladic, 74; Mycenaean town and trade, 233, 258, 263; tombs at, 300

15.28 **Sub-subentries in indented indexes.** In an indented index, sub-subentries are best run in (see example A below). If, in a particular index, running them in makes the index hard to use, they have to be indented more deeply than the subentries (example B). When the first method is used, runover lines need not be indented more than the standard two ems, already a fairly deep indentation. When the second is used, runover lines have to be indented three ems, which may result in some very short lines. See also 15.141, 15.142.

Example A (indented index: run-in sub-subentries)

nutritional analysis of bamboo, 72–81
  digestible energy, 94–96, 213–14, 222
  inorganic constituents: minerals, 81, 83–85, 89; silica (*see* silica levels in bamboo); total ash, 73, 79, 80, 91, 269, 270
  methods used, 72–73

organic constituents, 73–79, 269, 270; amino acids, 75–76, 86, 89; amino acids compared with other foods, 77; cellulose, 73, 78, 269, 270; crude protein, 73–75, 80, 89–91, 213, 269, 270; standard proximate analysis of, 78–80; vitamin C, 78, 79

Example B (indented index: sub-subentries indented)

nutritional analysis of bamboo, 72–81
  digestible energy, 94–96, 213–14, 222
  inorganic constituents
    minerals, 81, 83–85, 89
    silica (*see* silica levels in bamboo)
    total ash, 73, 79, 80, 91, 269, 270
    methods used, 72–73
  organic constituents, 73–79, 269, 270

    amino acids, 75–76, 86, 89
    amino acids compared with other foods, 77
    cellulose, 73, 78, 269, 270
    crude protein, 73–75, 80, 89–91, 213, 269, 270
    standard proximate analysis of, 78–80
    vitamin C, 78, 79

If sub-sub-subentries are required (which heaven forbid!), style B must be used, and they must be run in.

GENERAL PRINCIPLES OF INDEXING

15.29 **Style and usage in the index relative to the work.** Each index is a tool for one particular work. By the time the index is prepared, the style used in the work has long been determined, and the index must reflect that style. If British spelling has been used throughout the text, it must be used in the index. Shakspere in the text calls for Shakspere in the index. Hernando Cortez should not be indexed as Cortés. Older geographic terms should not be altered to their present form (Constantinople to Istanbul, Siam to Thailand, etc.). The use of accents and other diacritical marks must be observed exactly as in the text (Schönberg *not* Schoenberg). Only in the rare instance in which readers might not find information sought should a cross-reference be given. Any terms italicized or enclosed in quotation marks in the text should be treated similarly in the index. If inclusive numbers are given in full in the text (see 15.14; see also 9.64), that style should be used in the index.

15.30 **Choosing indexing terms.** The wording for all headings should be concise and logical. As far as possible, terms should be chosen according to the author's usage. If, for example, the author of a philosophical work uses *essence* to mean *being*, the main entry should be under *essence*, possibly with a cross-reference from *being*. If the terms are used interchangeably, the indexer may either choose one (in this case a cross-reference is imperative) or list both (see 15.16). An indexer relatively unfamiliar with the subject matter may find it useful to ask the author for a brief list of terms that must appear in the index, though such terms will usually suggest themselves as the indexer proceeds through the proofs. Common sense is the best guide. See also 15.21.

15.31 **Terms that should not be indexed.** Although proper names are an important element in most indexes, there are times when they should be ignored. In a work on the history of the automobile in the United States, for example, an author might write, "After World War II small sports cars like the British MG, often owned by returning veterans, began to make their appearance in college towns like Northampton, Massachusetts, and Ann Arbor, Michigan." An indexer should resist the temptation to index these place-names; the two towns mentioned have nothing to do with the theme of the work. The MG sports car, on the other hand, should be indexed, given the subject of the work. Similarly, names or terms that occur in passing references and scene-setting elements that are not essential to the theme of a work need not be indexed. (An exception might be made if certain readers of a publication would be likely to look for their own names in the index. Occasional vanity entries are not forbidden.)

WHAT PARTS OF A WORK TO INDEX

15.32   **Indexing the text, front matter, and back matter.** The entire text of a book, including substantive content in notes (see 15.33), should be indexed. Much of the front matter, however, is not indexable—title page, dedication, epigraphs, lists of illustrations and tables, and acknowledgments. A preface, or a foreword by someone other than the author of the work, may be indexed if it concerns the subject of the work and not simply how the work came to be written. Substantive material in an introduction, whether in the front matter or, more commonly, in the body of the work, is always indexed (for introduction versus preface, see 1.48). Appendixes should be indexed if they contain information that supplements the text, but not if they merely reproduce documents that are discussed in the text (the full text of a treaty, for example, or a questionnaire). Glossaries, bibliographies, and other such lists are usually not indexed.

15.33   **Indexing footnotes and endnotes.** Notes, whether footnotes or endnotes, should be indexed only if they continue or amplify discussion in the text (substantive notes). Notes that merely contain source citations documenting statements in the text (reference notes) need not be indexed. The same note may of course contain a mix of substantive, indexable content and source citations.

15.34   **Endnote locators in index entries.** Endnotes in printed works are referred to by page, the letter *n* (for *note*), and—extremely important—the note number, with no internal space (334n14). If two or more consecutive notes are referred to, two *n*'s and an en dash are used (e.g., 334nn14–16). Nonconsecutive notes on the same page are treated separately (334n14, 334n16, 334n19). If an index entry refers to numbered notes from more than one chapter that occur on the same page in the endnotes, it can be helpful to include the chapter number in parentheses after the note number, especially if two notes share the same number or where the notes might otherwise appear to be out of order.

15.35 **Footnote locators in index entries.** Footnotes in a printed work are generally referred to in the same way as endnotes. When a footnote is the only
one on the page, however, the note number (or symbol, if numbers are
not used) may be omitted (156n). Note numbers should never be omitted when several notes appear on the same page. (If symbols are used,
use the symbol: e.g., 156n*, 173n*, 173n†.) If there is indexable material
in a text passage and in a related footnote, only the page number need
be given. But if the text and the footnote materials are not connected,
both text and note should be cited (156, 156n, 278, 278n30).

15.36 **Indexing notes spanning more than one printed page.** For endnotes or
footnotes that continue onto another page, normally only the first page
number is given. But if the reference is specifically to a part of a note
that appears on the second page, the second page number should be
used. Referring to a succession of notes, however, may require inclusive
page numbers (e.g., 234–35nn19–23).

15.37 **Indexing parenthetical text citations.** Documentation given as parenthetical author-date citations in text is not normally indexed unless the
citation documents an otherwise unattributed statement in the text (see
15.33). Any author discussed in text should be indexed. In some fields
it is customary to index every author *named* in the text; check with the
publisher on the degree of inclusiveness required. In primarily legal
works, parenthetical case citations are usually indexed. See also 15.38.

15.38 **Indexing authors' names for an author index.** Author indexes are more
common in disciplines that use a variation of the author-date system
(see 13.102). Since most authors are cited in text by last name and date
only, full names must be sought in the reference list. Occasional dis-
crepancies between text and reference list, not caught in editing, have
to be sorted out or queried, adding to the time it takes to create an author index. Is L. W. Dinero, cited on page 345, the same person as Lauren Dinero, discussed on page 456? If so, should she be indexed as Dinero, Lauren W.? (Answer: Only if all or most authors are indexed with
full first names—a situation that may be determined by the reference
list.) Where a work by two or more authors is cited in text, the indexer
must determine whether each author named requires a separate en-

try. Should Jones, Smith, and Black share one index entry, or should three entries appear? And what about Jones et al.? Chicago recommends the following procedure: Make separate entries for each author whose name appears in text. Do not index those unfortunates whose names are concealed under *et al.* in text.

Text citations	*Index entries*
(Jones, Smith, and Black 1999)	Black, M. X., 366
(Sánchez et al. 2001)	Cruz, M. M., 435
(Sánchez, Cruz, et al. 2002)	Jones, E. J., 366
	Sánchez, J. G., 435, 657
	Smith, R. A., 366

15.39 **Indexing illustrations, tables, charts, and such.** Illustrative matter may be indexed if it is of particular importance to the discussion, especially when such items are not listed in or after the table of contents. References to illustrations may be set in italics (or boldface, if preferred); a headnote should then be inserted at the beginning of the index (see 15.140 for an example). Such references usually follow in page order.

reptilian brain, 199, 201–3, *202*, 341,
   477, 477–81

Alternatively, references to tables may be denoted by *t*, to figures by *f*, plates by *pl*, or whatever works (all set in roman, with no space following the page number). Add an appropriate headnote (e.g., "The letter *t* following a page number denotes a table"). If the number of an illustration is essential, it is safer to use *table*, *fig.*, and so on, with no comma following the page number.

authors and printers, 69, 208t, 209t,
   210f
titi monkeys, 88 table 5, 89–90, 122–
   25, 122 fig. 7

INDEXING PROPER NAMES AND VARIANTS

15.40 **Choosing between variant names.** When proper names appear in the text in more than one form, or in an incomplete form, the indexer must decide which form to use for the main entry and which for the cross-reference (if any) and occasionally must furnish identifying information not given in the text. Few indexes need to provide the kind of detail found in biographical or geographic dictionaries, though reference works of that kind will help in decision-making.

15.41 **Indexing familiar forms of personal names.** The full form of personal names should be indexed as they have become widely known. (Any variant spelling preferred in the text, however, must likewise be preferred in the index; see 15.29.) Note that brackets are used in the following examples to distinguish Chicago's editorial glosses from parenthetical tags such as those in some of the examples elsewhere in this section, which would actually appear in a published index.

Cervantes, Miguel de [*not* Cervantes Saavedra, Miguel de]
Fisher, M. F. K. [*not* Fisher, Mary Frances Kennedy]

London, Jack [*not* London, John Griffith]
Poe, Edgar Allan [*not* Poe, E. A., *or* Poe, Edgar A.]

But in a work devoted to, say, M. F. K. Fisher or Cervantes, the full form of the name should appear in the index.

15.42 **Indexing pseudonyms, stage names, and other alternative names.** Persons who have used pseudonyms or other professional names are usually listed under their real names (assuming both forms of the name appear in the indexed work). If the pseudonym has become a household word, however, it should be used as the main entry, with the real name in parentheses if it is relevant to the work; a cross-reference is seldom necessary. If there is any doubt about adding an alternative form of a name that does not appear in the text (particularly for a living person who is no longer known by that alternative form, as in the case of a deadname), it should be omitted.

Æ. *See* Russell, George William
Ouida. *See* Ramée, Marie Louise de la
Ramée, Marie Louise de la (pseud. Ouida)
Russell, George William (pseud. Æ)
but
Molière (Jean-Baptiste Poquelin)
Monroe, Marilyn (Norma Jean Baker)
Rihanna (Robyn Rihanna Fenty)
Twain, Mark (Samuel Langhorne Clemens)
Voltaire (François-Marie Arouet)

15.43 **Indexing persons with the same name.** Persons with the same name should be distinguished by a middle initial (if either has one) or by a parenthetical tag.

Campbell, James	Field, David Dudley (lawyer)
Campbell, James B.	Pitt, William (the elder)
Field, David Dudley (clergyman)	Pitt, William (the younger)

In works that include many persons with the same last name (often a family name), parenthetical identifications are useful. For example, in *Two Lucky People,* by Milton Friedman and Rose D. Friedman (University of Chicago Press, 1998), the following identifications appear:

Friedman, David (son of MF and RDF)	Friedman, Milton (MF)
Friedman, Helen (sister of MF)	Friedman, Rose Director (RDF)
Friedman, Janet (daughter of MF and RDF)	Friedman, Sarah Ethel Landau (mother of MF)

15.44 **Indexing married women's names.** A married woman who is known variously by her birth name or by her married name, depending on context, should be indexed by her birth name unless the married name is the more familiar. A married woman who uses both birth and married names together is usually indexed by her married name (unless the two names are hyphenated). Parenthetical clarifications or cross-references may be supplied as necessary.

Marinoff, Fania (married to Carl Van Vechten)
Sutherland, Joan (married to Richard Bonynge)
Van Vechten, Fania. *See* Marinoff, Fania
but
Besant, Annie (née Wood)
Browning, Elizabeth Barrett
Clinton, Hillary Rodham

15.45 **Indexing monarchs, popes, and the like.** Monarchs, popes, and others who are known by their official names, often including a Roman numeral, should be indexed under the official name. Identifying tags may be omitted or expanded as appropriate in a particular work.

Anne, Queen	Benedict XVI (pope)	Charles III (king)

15.46 **Indexing princes, dukes, and other titled persons.** Princes and princesses are usually indexed under their given names. Dukes, earls, and the like are indexed under the title. A cross-reference may be needed where a title differs from a family name.

Catherine, Princess of Wales
Cooper, Anthony Ashley. *See* Shaftesbury, 7th Earl of

Shaftesbury, 7th Earl of (Anthony
  Ashley Cooper)
William, Prince of Wales

Unless necessary for identification, the titles *Lord* and *Lady* are best omitted from an index, since their use with given names is far from simple. *Sir* and *Dame*, while easier to cope with, are also unnecessary in most indexes. Brackets are used here to denote Chicago's editorial glosses (see 15.41).

Churchill, Winston [*or* Churchill, Sir Winston]
Hess, Myra [*or* Hess, Dame Myra]
Thatcher, Margaret [even if referred to as Lady Thatcher in text]

But in a work dealing with the nobility, or a historical work such as *The Lisle Letters* (University of Chicago Press, 1981), from which the following examples are taken, titles may be an appropriate or needed element in index entries. The last two examples illustrate distinctions for which expert advice may be needed.

Arundell, Sir John
Audley, Thomas Lord
Grey, Lady Jane ["Lady Jane Grey"
  in text]

Whethill, Elizabeth (Muston), Lady
  ["Lady Whethill" in text]

15.47 **Clerical titles in index entries.** Like titles of nobility, such abbreviations as *Rev.* or *Msgr.* should be used only when necessary for identification (see 15.46).

Councell, George E. (rector of the Church of the Holy Spirit)
Cranmer, Thomas (archbishop of Canterbury)
Jaki, Rev. Stanley S.
Manniere, Msgr. Charles L.

15.48 **Academic titles and degrees in index entries.** Academic titles such as *Prof.* and *Dr.*, used before a name, are not retained in indexing, nor are abbreviations of degrees such as *PhD* or *MD*.

15.49 **"Jr.," "Sr.," "III," and the like in index entries.** Abbreviations such as *Jr.* are retained in indexing but are placed after the given name and preceded by a comma (see also 6.46).

King, Martin Luther, Jr.
Stevenson, Adlai E., III

15.50 **Indexing saints.** Saints are indexed under their given names unless another name is equally well or better known. Parenthetical identifications or cross-references (as well as discretion) may be needed. See also 15.82.

Aquinas. *See* Thomas Aquinas, Saint   Chrysostom, Saint John
Borromeo, Saint Charles   Thomas, Saint (the apostle)
Catherine of Siena, Saint   Thomas Aquinas, Saint

15.51 **Indexing persons whose full names are unknown.** Persons referred to in the work by first or last names only should be parenthetically identified if the full name is unavailable.

John (Smith's shipmate on *Stella*)
Thaxter (family physician)

15.52 **Indexing incomplete names or names alluded to in text.** Even if only an epithet or a shortened form of a name is used in the text, the index should give the full form.

Text	*Index*
the lake	Michigan, Lake
the bay	San Francisco Bay
the Village	Greenwich Village
the Great Emancipator	Lincoln, Abraham

15.53 **Indexing confusing names.** When the same name is used of more than one entity, identifying tags should be provided.

New York (city) *or* New York City
New York (state) *or* New York State

15.54 **Indexing abbreviations.** Organizations that are widely known under their abbreviations should be indexed and alphabetized according to the abbreviations. Parenthetical glosses, cross-references, or both should be added if the abbreviations, however familiar to the indexer, may not be known to all readers of the particular work. Lesser-known organizations are better indexed under the full name, with a cross-reference from the abbreviation if it is used frequently in the work. See also 15.16.

EEC (European Economic Community)
MLA. *See* Modern Language Association
NATO

INDEXING TITLES OF PUBLICATIONS AND OTHER WORKS

15.55 **Typographic treatment for indexed titles of works.** Titles of newspapers, books, journals, stories, poems, artwork, musical compositions, and such should be treated typographically as they appear in text—whether italicized, set in roman and enclosed in quotation marks, or simply capitalized (see also 8.157–204).

15.56 **Indexing newspaper titles.** English-language newspapers should be indexed as they are generally known, whether or not the city of publication appears on the masthead. The name is italicized, as in text. An initial *The* included in the text may be omitted as a matter of editorial expediency (see also 8.172, 15.59). If necessary, a city of publication may be added in parentheses following the title.

Chicago Sun-Times   *Plain Dealer* (Cleveland)
Christian Science Monitor   *Times* (London)
New York Times   *Wall Street Journal*

For newspapers published in languages other than English, any article (*Le, Die,* etc.) follows the name in a main index entry, separated by a comma (but see 15.60). The city of publication may be added parenthetically, following the title.

Akhbar, Al- (Cairo)   *Prensa, La* (Buenos Aires)
Monde, Le (Paris)   *Süddeutsche Zeitung, Die*

15.57 **Indexing magazine and journal titles.** Magazines and journals are indexed in the same way as newspapers (see 15.56). An initial *The* included in the text may be omitted as a matter of editorial expediency (see also 8.172, 15.59). The article is retained, however, following the name, for non-English titles (but see 15.60).

JAMA (*Journal of the American Medical Association*)
New England Journal of Medicine
Spiegel, Der
Time (magazine)

15.58   **Indexing authored titles of works.** A published work, a musical composition, or a piece of art that merits its own main entry should also be indexed under the name of its creator, often as a subentry. The main heading is followed by the creator's name in parentheses (except in an index in which all titles cited have the same creator).

> *Look Homeward, Angel* (Wolfe), 34–37
> Wolfe, Thomas: childhood, 6–8;
>   early literary influences on, 7–10;
>   *Look Homeward, Angel,* 34–37; and
>   Maxwell Perkins, 30–41

Several works by a single creator are sometimes treated as subentries under a new main heading, following a main entry on the creator. This device is best employed when many works as well as many topics are listed. Separate main entries may also be included for the works.

> Mozart, Wolfgang Amadeus, 49–51, 55–56; early musical compositions of, 67–72, 74–80; to Italy with father, 85–92; Salzburg appointment, 93–95; in Vienna, 98–105
>
> Mozart, Wolfgang Amadeus, works of: *La clemenza di Tito,* 114; *Don Giovanni,* 115; *Idomeneo,* 105–6; *Jupiter Symphony,* 107; *The Magic Flute,* 111–13; *The Marriage of Figaro,* 109–12

15.59   **Indexing English-language titles beginning with an article.** In titles beginning with *A, An,* or *The,* the article is traditionally placed at the end of the title, following a comma, when the title forms a main heading. (Note, however, that an initial *The* may be omitted from the title of a periodical; see 15.56, 15.57.) When such a title occurs as a subheading, it appears in its normal position in a run-in index, where inversion would be clumsy and unnecessary, but is inverted in an indented index for easier alphabetic scanning.

> *Professor and the Madman, The* (Winchester), 209–11
> Winchester, Simon: *Pacific,* 190–95; *The Professor and the Madman,* 209–11; *The River at the Center of the World,* 211–15
>
> Winchester, Simon
>   *Pacific,* 190–95
>   *Professor and the Madman, The,* 209–11
>   *River at the Center of the World, The,* 211–15

Subtitles in index entries and subentries are normally omitted (see 15.63). If the subtitle is retained for any reason, an initial article follows the main title in a main index entry or an indented subentry (but appears in its normal position in a run-in subentry).

> Vampire, His Kith and Kin, The: A
>   Critical Edition, 88–91
> See also 15.64.

15.60 **Indexing non-English titles beginning with an article.** Since initial articles in non-English titles sometimes modify the following word, they are usually retained in an index. In publications intended for a general audience, especially those that mention only a few such titles, it is acceptable to list the titles in the index exactly as they appear in the text, without inversion and alphabetized according to the article.

> *Eine kleine Nachtmusik* (Mozart), 23
> *La bohème* (Puccini), 211

In a more specialized work, or any work intended for readers who are likely to be well versed in the languages of any non-English titles mentioned in the text, the titles may be inverted as they are in English (see 15.59). According to this practice, the articles follow the rest of the title in main entries but remain, as in English titles, in their normal position in run-in subentries. In both positions, the articles are ignored in alphabetizing.

> *bohème, La* (Puccini), 211
> *clemenza de Tito, La* (Mozart), 22
> *kleine Nachtmusik, Eine* (Mozart), 23
> Mozart, Wolfgang Amadeus: *La*
>   *clemenza de Tito*, 22; *Eine kleine*
>   *Nachtmusik*, 23
> *trovatore, Il* (Verdi), 323
> but
> "Un deux trois" (Luboff), 47 [alpha-
>   betize under *U*]

An indexer unfamiliar with the language of a title should make sure that the article is indeed an article and not a number (see last example above). French *un* and *une* and German *ein* and *eine*, for example, can mean *one* as well as *a*. See also 11.8–12.

15.61 **Indexing titles beginning with a preposition.** Unlike articles, prepositions beginning a title always remain in their original position and are never dropped, whether in English or non-English titles—nor are they ignored in alphabetizing (but see 15.76).

For Whom the Bell Tolls
Por quién doblan las campanas

15.62   **Indexing titles ending with a question mark or exclamation point.** A question mark or exclamation point at the end of an indexed title should be followed by a comma wherever a comma is called for by the syntax of the heading. See also 6.134, 15.102.

Carver, Raymond, 23–27, 101, 143–44;
"Are You a Doctor?," 25; *Will You*
Please Be Quiet, Please?, 25–27, 143.
See also Iowa Writers' Workshop

15.63   **Subtitles in index entries.** Subtitles of books or articles are omitted both in main headings and in subheadings unless essential for identification.

ALPHABETIZING

15.64   **Alphabetizing main headings — the basic rule.** To exploit the virtues of alphabetizing and thus ease the way for readers, the first word in a main heading should always determine the location of the entry. This principle occasionally entails inversion of the main heading. Thus, for example, *A Tale of Two Cities* is inverted as *Tale of Two Cities, A* and alphabetized under *T*, where readers would be inclined to look first. See also 15.9, 15.59, 15.60. For subentries, see 15.76–78.

15.65   **Computerized sorting.** Few computerized sorting options—and none of the standard options available with ordinary word processors—will perfectly conform to either system of alphabetization as described here. Those using a word processor to create their index will need to edit the finished product for the glitches and inconsistencies that invariably remain. Note that word processors typically produce a version of the word-by-word system, which Chicago now prefers (see 15.66). Some dedicated indexing programs, on the other hand, have been specially programmed to sort according to either the word-by-word or letter-by-letter system in conformance with the detailed guidelines presented in this section. See also 15.113.

Letter by Letter or Word by Word?

15.66   **Two systems of alphabetizing — an overview.** The two principal modes of alphabetizing—or sorting—indexes are the *letter-by-letter* and the *word-*

by-word systems. A choice between the two should be made before indexing begins, though occasionally an indexer will find, as indexing progresses, that a change from one to the other is appropriate. (Such a change would of course need to be applied to the entire index.) Dictionaries are arranged letter by letter, library catalogs word by word (though online catalogs can usually be sorted by other criteria, such as format, date, availability, or relevance to a search). In an index with many open compounds starting with the same word, the word-by-word system is generally easier for users. For that reason, and because word processors typically sort word by word, Chicago now prefers the word-by-word system (a departure from previous editions) but will not normally impose it on a well-prepared index that has been arranged letter by letter. Both systems have their advantages and disadvantages, and few users are confused by either. Most people simply scan an alphabetic block until they find what they are looking for. The indexer must understand both systems, however, and the following paragraphs offer guidelines for each. For a fuller discussion, consult Nancy Mulvany, *Indexing Books* (bibliog. 2.5).

15.67 **The letter-by-letter system.** In the letter-by-letter system, alphabetizing continues up to the first parenthesis or comma; it then starts again after the punctuation point. Spaces and all other punctuation marks are ignored. The order of precedence is one word, word followed by a parenthesis, word followed by a comma, then (ignoring spaces and other punctuation) word followed by a number, and word followed by letters.

15.68 **The word-by-word system.** In the word-by-word system, alphabetizing continues only up to the end of the first word (counting an abbreviation or a hyphenated compound as one word), using subsequent words only when additional headings begin with the same word. As in the letter-by-letter system, alphabetizing continues up to the first parenthesis or comma; it then starts again after the punctuation point. The order of precedence is one word, word followed by a parenthesis, word followed by a comma, word followed by a space, then (ignoring other punctuation) word followed by a number, and word followed by letters. The index to this manual, in accordance with Chicago's new preference, is arranged word by word.

15.69 **The two systems compared.** In both systems a parenthesis or comma (in that order) interrupts the alphabetizing, and other punctuation marks (hyphens, slashes, quotation marks, periods, etc.) are ignored. The columns below illustrate the similarities and differences between the systems.

Letter by letter	Word by word
NEW (Neighbors Ever Watchful)	N. Ewing & Sons
NEW (Now End War)	NEW (Neighbors Ever Watchful)
New, Arthur	NEW (Now End War)
New, Zoe	New, Arthur
new-12 compound	New, Zoe
newborn	New Deal
newcomer	new economics
New Deal	New England
new economics	new math
newel	New Thorndale
New England	new town
"new-fangled notions"	New Year's Day
Newfoundland	new-12 compound
N. Ewing & Sons	newborn
newlyweds	newcomer
new math	newel
new/old continuum	"new-fangled notions"
news, lamentable	Newfoundland
News, Networks, and the Arts	newlyweds
newsboy	new/old continuum
news conference	news, lamentable
newsletter	*News, Networks, and the Arts*
News of the World (Queen)	news conference
news release	*News of the World* (Queen)
newt	news release
NEWT (Northern Estuary Wind	newsboy
Tunnel)	newsletter
New Thorndale	newt
new town	NEWT (Northern Estuary Wind
New Year's Day	Tunnel)

General Rules of Alphabetizing

15.70   **Alphabetizing items with the same name.** When a person, a place, and a thing have the same name, they are arranged in normal alphabetical order.

hoe, garden	London, England
Hoe, Robert	London, Jack

Common sense must be exercised. If Amy London and Carolyn Hoe were to appear in the same index as illustrated above, adjustments in the other entries would be needed.

garden hoe   London (England)
hoe. *See* garden hoe   London, Amy
Hoe, Carolyn   London, Jack
Hoe, Robert

15.71   **Alphabetizing initials versus spelled-out names.** Initials used in place of a given name come before any spelled-out name beginning with the same letter.

Oppenheimer, J. Robert   Oppenheimer, K. T.
Oppenheimer, James N.   Oppenheimer, Katharine S.

15.72   **Alphabetizing abbreviations.** Acronyms, initialisms, and most abbreviations are alphabetized as they appear, not according to their spelled-out versions, and are interspersed alphabetically among entries. See also 15.54, 15.82.

faculty clubs   NATO
FBI   North Pole
Feely, John   NOW (National Organization for Women)
LBJ. *See* Johnson, Lyndon B.

Two exceptions: An ampersand (&) may be treated as if spelled out, and an at sign (@), which normally can be treated like the letter *a*, may be ignored as part of a screen name.

15.73   **Alphabetizing headings beginning with numerals.** Isolated entries beginning with numerals are alphabetized as though spelled out. (For numerals occurring in the middle of a heading, see 15.69, 15.74.)

1984 (Orwell) [*alphabetized as* nineteen eighty-four]
125th Street [*alphabetized as* one hundred twenty-fifth street]
10 Downing Street [*alphabetized as* ten downing street]

If many such entries occur in an index, they may be listed together in numerical order at the beginning of the index, before the *A*s.

15.74   **Alphabetizing similar headings containing numerals.** When two or more similar headings with numerals occur together, they are ordered numerically, regardless of how they would be spelled out.

Henry III   L7   section 9
Henry IV   L44   section 44
Henry V   L50   section 77

The *L* entries above would be placed at the beginning of the *L* section. See also 15.69.

15.75 **Alphabetizing accented letters.** Words beginning with or including accented letters are alphabetized as though they were unaccented. (Note that this rule is intended for English-language indexes that include some non-English words. The alphabetizing practices of other languages are not relevant in such instances.)

Ubeda	Schoenberg
Über den Gipfel	Schomberg
Ubina	Schönborn

This system, more than adequate for most English-language indexes, may need to be supplemented by more comprehensive systems for indexes that contain many terms in other languages. The Unicode Consortium has developed extensive specifications and recommendations for sorting (or collating) the characters used in many of the world's languages. For more information, refer to the latest version of the *Unicode Collation Algorithm*, published by the Unicode Consortium (bibliog. 5). See also 11.2.

Subentries

15.76 **Alphabetical order of subentries.** Introductory articles, prepositions, and conjunctions are disregarded in alphabetizing subentries (but see 15.61), whether the subentries are run in or indented. To preserve the alphabetic logic of the keywords, avoid substantive introductory words at the beginnings of subheadings (e.g., *"relations* with," *"views* on").

> Churchill, Winston: as anti-Fascist, 369; on Curzon line, 348, 379; and de Gaulle, 544n4

In indented style, where alphabetizing functions more visually, it may be better to dispense with such introductory words or to invert the headings, amplifying them as needed. The subheadings from the first example could be edited for an indented index as follows:

> Churchill, Winston
> anti-Fascism of, 369
> Curzon line, views on, 348, 379
> de Gaulle, relations with, 544n4

15.77 **Numerical order of subentries.** Occasional subentries demand numerical order even if others in the same index (but not the same entry) are alphabetized.

> Daley, Richard J. (mayor): third term,
>   205; fourth term, 206–7
> flora, alpine: at 1,000-meter level, 46,
>   130–35; at 1,500-meter level, 146–
>   54; at 2,000-meter level, 49, 164–74

15.78 **Chronological order of subentries.** In a run-in index, the subentries for the subject of a biography may be arranged chronologically rather than alphabetically so as to provide a quick summary of the subject's career and to avoid, for example, a subheading "death of" near the beginning of the entry. This system should be used with caution, however, and only when the biographical and chronological logic is obvious from the subentries.

Personal Names

15.79 **Indexing names with particles.** In alphabetizing family names containing particles, the indexer must consider the individual's personal preference (if known) as well as traditional and national usages. The biographical entries in Merriam-Webster's dictionaries (bibliog. 3.1) are authoritative for well-known persons long deceased; library catalogs and encyclopedias are far broader in scope. Cross-references are often advisable (see 15.17). Note the wide variations in the following list of actual names arranged alphabetically as they might appear in an index. See also 8.5, 15.83, 15.92.

> Beauvoir, Simone de   di Leonardo, Micaela
> Ben-Gurion, David   Keere, Pieter van den
> Costa, Uriel da   La Fontaine, Jean de
> da Cunha, Euclides   Leonardo da Vinci
> D'Amato, Alfonse   Medici, Lorenzo de'
> de Gaulle, Charles   Van Rensselaer, Stephen

Charles de Gaulle is a good example of the opportunity for occasional editorial discretion: *Merriam-Webster* and the Library of Congress, for example, list the French statesman under "Gaulle"; the entry in *American Heritage* is under "de Gaulle"—the usage normally preferred by Chicago.

15.80   **Indexing compound names.** Compound family names, with or without hyphens, are usually alphabetized according to the first element (but see 15.44). See also 8.7, 8.12, 15.91, 15.92.

Lloyd George, David   Sackville-West, Victoria
Mies van der Rohe, Ludwig   Teilhard de Chardin, Pierre

15.81   **Indexing names with "Mac," "Mc," or "O'."** Names beginning with *Mac* or *Mc* are alphabetized letter by letter, as they appear.

Macalister, Donald   Madison, James
MacAlister, Paul   McAllister, Ward
Macauley, Catharine   McAuley, Catherine
Macmillan, Harold   McMillan, Edwin M.

Names beginning with *O'* are alphabetized as if the apostrophe were missing.

Onassis, Aristotle   O'Neill, Eugene   Ongaro, Francesco dall'

15.82   **Indexing names with "Saint."** A family name in the form of a saint's name is alphabetized according to how the name is spelled, whether *Saint*, *San*, *St.*, or however. A cross-reference may be useful if *Saint* and *St.* are far apart in an index. See also 15.50, 15.101.

Sainte-Beuve, Charles-Augustin   San Martin, José de
Saint-Gaudens, Augustus   St. Denis, Ruth
Saint-Saëns, Camille   St. Laurent, Louis Stephen

15.83   **Indexing Arabic names.** Modern Arabic names consisting of one or more given names followed by a surname present no problem.

Himsi, Ahmad Hamid   Sadat, Anwar

Arabic surnames prefixed by *al* or *el* (the) are alphabetized under the element following the particle; the article is treated like *de* in many French names.

Hakim, Tawfiq al-   Jamal, Muhammad Hamid al-

Names beginning with *Abu*, *Abd*, and *Ibn*, elements as integral to the names as *Mc* or *Fitz*, are alphabetized under those elements.

Abu Zafar Nadvi, Syed   Ibn Saud, Abdul Aziz

Context and readership may suggest cross-references. For example, in an index to a work likely to have readers unfamiliar with Arabic names, a cross-reference may be useful (e.g., "al-Farabi. *See* Farabi, al-").

15.84 **Indexing Burmese names.** Burmese persons are usually known by a given name of one or more elements and should be indexed under the first element. If the name is preceded in text by a term of respect (*U, Daw,* etc.), that term either is omitted or follows in the index.

Aung San Suu Kyi [alphabetize under *A*]
Thant, U [alphabetize under *T*]

15.85 **Indexing Chinese names.** Chinese names should be indexed as spelled in the work, whether in the Pinyin or the Wade-Giles system. Cross-references are needed only if alternative forms are used in the text. Since the family name precedes the given name in Chinese usage, names are not inverted in the index, and no comma is used.

Li Bai [Pinyin; alphabetize under *L*]
Mao Tse-tung [Wade-Giles; alphabetize under *M*]

Persons of Chinese ancestry or origin who have adopted the Western practice of giving the family name last are indexed with inversion and a comma.

Kung, H. H.   Tsou, Tang

Note that strict alphabetical order in an index that includes entries for multiple people who share the same family name can be modified if some of the names are inverted and others are not. For example, the following order would be preferred as an exception in both word-by-word and letter-by-letter order:

Li Jinghan
Li, Lillian
Liang Qichao
not this (strict word by word):
Li, Lillian
Li Jinghan
Liang Qichao
and not this (strict letter by letter):
Li, Lillian
Liang Qichao
Li Jinghan

Elsewhere in the same index, any name that is not inverted may be treated similarly for the sake of consistency.

15.86 **Indexing Hungarian names.** In Hungarian practice the family name precedes the given name—for example, Bartók Béla, Molnár Ferenc. In English contexts, however, such names are usually inverted; in an index they are therefore reinverted, with a comma added.

Bartók, Béla Molnár, Ferenc

Family names beginning with an initial should be indexed under the initial (see also 8.14).

É. Kiss, Katalin

15.87 **Indexing Indian names.** Modern Indian names generally appear with the family name last and are indexed accordingly. As with all names, the personal preference of the individual as well as usage should be observed.

Gandhi, Mohandas Karamchand
Krishna Menon, V. K.
Narayan, R. K.

15.88 **Indexing Indonesian names.** Usage varies. Some Indonesians (especially Javanese) use only a single, given name. Others use more than one name; even though the given name comes first, these are often indexed like Chinese names, with no inversion or punctuation (see third and fourth examples below). Indonesians with Muslim names and certain others whose names may include a title or an honorific are indexed by the final element, with inversion. The indexer must therefore ascertain how a person's full name is referred to in text and which part of the name is used for a short reference.

Habibi, B. J.   Suharto
Hatta, Mohammed   Sukarno
Marzuki Darusman   Suryokusumo, Wiyono
Pramoedya Ananta Toer

15.89 **Indexing Japanese names.** In Japanese usage the family name precedes the given name; names are therefore not inverted in the index, and no comma is used. If the name is westernized, as it often is by authors writing in English, the family name comes last. The indexer must therefore

33

make certain which practice is followed in the text so that the family name always appears first in the index.

Tajima Yumiko [alphabetize under *T*]
Yoshida Shigeru [alphabetize under *Y*]
but
Kurosawa, Noriaki [referred to in text as Noriaki Kurosawa]

15.90   **Indexing Korean names.** In Korean usage the family name precedes the given name, and this is how it is usually presented even in English-language contexts. Persons of Korean origin living in the West, however, often invert this order. The indexer must therefore make certain which practice is followed in the text so that the family name appears first, with or without inversion, in the index.

Kim Dae-jung [alphabetize under *K*]
Oh Jung-hee [alphabetize under *O*]
but
Lee, Chang-rae [referred to in text as Chang-rae Lee]

15.91   **Indexing Portuguese names.** Portuguese surnames, unlike Spanish surnames (see 15.92), are indexed by the last element. This does not include the designations *Filho* (son), *Neto* (grandson), and *Júnior*, which always follow the second family name.

Câmara Júnior, José Mattoso
Jucá Filho, Cândido
Martins, Luciana de Lima
Silva Neto, Serafim da
Vasconcellos, J. Leite de

Where both Portuguese and Spanish names appear in the same context, cross-references may be necessary.

15.92   **Indexing Spanish names.** In Spain and in some Latin American countries a double family name is often used, of which the first element is the father's family name and the second the mother's birth name (*her* father's family name). The two names are sometimes joined by *y* (and). Such compound names are alphabetized under the first element. Cross-references will often be needed, especially if the person is generally known under the second element or if the indexer is uncertain where to place the main entry. *Merriam-Webster* is a good guide for persons listed

34

there. Where many Spanish names appear, an indexer not conversant with Spanish or Latin American culture should seek help.

García Lorca, Federico
Lorca, Federico García. *See* García Lorca, Federico
Ortega y Gasset, José
Sánchez Mendoza, Juana

When the particle *de* appears in a Spanish name, the family name, under which the person is indexed, may be either the preceding or the following name (depending in part on how a person is known). If it is not clear from the text and the name is not in *Merriam-Webster* or otherwise widely known, a cross-reference will be needed.

Balboa, Vasco Núñez de
Esquivel de Sánchez, María
Fernández de Navarrete, Juan
Fernández de Oviedo, Gonzalo

Traditionally, a married woman replaced her mother's family name with her husband's (first) family name, sometimes preceded by *de*. Her name should be alphabetized, however, by the first family name (her father's).

Mendoza de Peña, María Carmen [woman's name after marriage]
Mendoza Salinas, María Carmen [woman's name before marriage]
Peña Montalvo, Juan Alberto [husband's name]

In telephone directories and elsewhere, some women appear under the husband's family name, but this is not a recommended bibliographic or indexing practice. Many modern women in Spanish-speaking countries no longer take the husband's family name. See also 8.12.

15.93 **Indexing Thai names.** Although family names are used in Thailand, Thai persons are normally known by their given names, which come first, as in English names. The name is often alphabetized under the first name, but practice varies. Seek expert help.

Sarit Thanarat [*or* Thanarat, Sarit]
Sivaraksa, Sulak [*or* Sulak Sivaraksa]
Supachai Panitchpakdi

15.94 **Indexing Vietnamese names.** Vietnamese names consist of three elements, the family name being the first. Since Vietnamese persons are usually referred to by the last part of their given names (Premier Diem, General Giap), they are best indexed under that form.

Diem, Ngo Dinh [*cross-reference under* Ngo Dinh Diem]
Giap, Vo Nguyen [*cross-reference under* Vo Nguyen Giap]

15.95 **Indexing other Asian names.** Throughout Asia, many names derive from Arabic, Chinese, the European languages, and other languages, regardless of where the bearers of the names were born. In the Philippines, for example, names follow a Western order, giving precedence to the family name, though the names themselves may be derived from local languages. In some parts of Asia, titles denoting status form part of a name as it appears in written work and must be dealt with appropriately. When the standard reference works do not supply an answer, query the author.

Names of Organizations and Businesses

15.96 **Omission of article in indexed names of organizations.** In indexing organizations whose names begin with *the* (which would be lowercased in running text), the article is omitted.

Beatles (band)   Unicode Consortium   University of Chicago

15.97 **Indexing personal names as corporate names.** When used as names of businesses or other organizations, full personal names are not inverted, and the corporate name is alphabetized under the first name or initials. An organization widely known by the family name, however, should be indexed under that name. In both instances, cross-references may be appropriate.

A. G. Edwards & Sons, Inc. [alphabetize under *A*]
Penney, J. C. *See* J. C. Penney Company, Inc.
Saphir, Kurt. *See* Kurt Saphir Pianos, Inc.
but
John G. Shedd Aquarium. *See* Shedd Aquarium

A personal name and the name of that person's company should be indexed separately.

J. S. Morgan & Company, 45–48. *See
  also* Morgan, Junius S.
Morgan, Junius S., 39, 42–44; J. S.
  Morgan & Company, 45–48

Names of Places

15.98   **Indexing names beginning with "Mount," "Lake," and such.** Proper names of mountains, lakes, and so forth that begin with a generic name are usually inverted and alphabetized under the nongeneric name. If the generic term is from another language, however, it can usually be left as is. If inverted (as in an index with more than a few such entries), it may be helpful to explain the decision in a headnote—for example, "Names beginning with *Mauna* (Mountain) have been inverted, as in 'Kea, Mauna.'" For isolated instances, double posting under both forms may be the better option (see also 15.16). A name that has recently changed may include a cross-reference under the old form of the name; if the older form occurs in the text (as in a direct quotation), this fact should be mentioned in parentheses after the main entry.

Denali (*also as* Mount McKinley)
Geneva, Lake
Japan, Sea of
McKinley, Mount. *See* Denali
but
Loch Ness
Mauna Kea
Sierra Nevada

Names of cities or towns beginning with topographic elements, as well as islands known as "Isle of . . . ," are alphabetized under the first element.

Isle of Pines   Mount Vernon, NY
Isle of Wight   Valley Forge
Lake Geneva, WI

15.99   **Indexing names beginning with the definite article.** Aside from a very few cities such as The Hague (unless the Dutch form *Den Haag* is used; see 15.100) and The Dalles, where *The* is part of the formal name and thus capitalized, an initial *the* used informally with place-names is omitted in indexing. See also 8.46.

Bronx	Loop (Chicago's downtown)	Ozarks
Hague, The	Netherlands	Philippines

15.100 **Indexing names beginning with non-English definite articles.** Names of places beginning with definite articles such as *El, Le, La,* and the like, whether in English- or non-English-speaking countries, are alphabetized according to the article.

Den Haag	La Mancha
El Dorado	Le Havre
El Paso	Les Baux-de-Provence
La Crosse	Los Alamos

15.101 **Indexing names of places beginning with "Saint."** Names of places beginning with *Saint, Sainte, St.,* or *Ste.* should be indexed as they appear in the text—that is, abbreviated only if abbreviated in text. Like personal names, they are alphabetized as they appear. Cross-references may be appropriate (e.g., "Saint. *See* St.," or vice versa). Note that French hyphenates place-names with *Saint.* See also 10.35, 11.28.

Saint-Cloud (in France)	St. Louis
Sainte-Foy	St. Vincent Island
Saint-Luc	Ste. Genevieve
St. Cloud (in Florida)	

PUNCTUATING INDEXES: A SUMMARY

15.102 **Comma in index entries.** In both run-in and indented indexes, when a main heading is followed immediately by locators (usually page or paragraph numbers; see 15.12), a comma appears before the first locator. Commas appear between locators. Commas are also used when a heading is an inversion or when a main heading is qualified, without subentries. The second example below illustrates three uses of the comma. For the role of commas in alphabetizing, see 15.69.

lighthouses, early history of, 40–42
Sabba da Castiglione, Monsignor,
      209, 337; on cosmetics, 190, 195, 198

15.103 **Colon in index entries.** In a run-in index, when a main heading is followed immediately by subentries, a colon appears before the first subheading. In an indented index, no punctuation is used after the main heading. A colon is also used in a cross-reference to a subentry. See also 15.20.

Maya: art of, 236–43; cities of, 178.   Maya
   See also Yucatán: Maya   art of, 236–43
                                    cities of, 178
                                    See also Yucatán: Maya

15.104   **Semicolon in index entries.** When subentries or sub-subentries are run in, they are separated by semicolons. Cross-references, if more than one, are also separated by semicolons.

astronomy: Galileo's works on, 20–21,
   22–23, 24; skills needed in, 548–49.
  See also Brahe, Tycho; comets;
  Flamsteed, John

15.105   **Period in index entries.** In a run-in index a period is used only before *See* (or *See under*) or *See also* (or *See also under*). In an indented index a period is used only before *See*. When a *see* or *see also* reference in parentheses follows a subheading or a subentry in either a run-in or an indented index, no period is used. No period follows the final word of any entry. For examples, see 15.17, 15.19, 15.20, 15.142.

15.106   **Parentheses in index headings.** Parentheses enclose identifying or supplementary information. For the role of parentheses in alphabetizing, see 15.69.

Charles I (king of England)
Charles I (king of Portugal)
Of Human Bondage (Maugham)

15.107   **Em dash in index entries.** For use of the em dash in run-in indexes that require occasional sub-subentries, see example B in 15.27.

15.108   **En dash in index entries.** The en dash is used for page ranges and all other inclusive locators (e.g., "dogs, 135–42"). For abbreviating inclusive numbers in indexes, see 15.14. See also 6.83, the index to this manual, and examples throughout this chapter.

THE MECHANICS OF INDEXING

Before Indexing Begins: Tools and Decisions

15.109 **Preliminary indexing work and when to begin.** Although some planning can be done at the manuscript stage, most indexes are prepared as soon as a work is in final, paginated form, or "page proofs." It is crucial, in fact, that indexing not begin until pagination is final. For indexes in which the locators are paragraph or section numbers rather than page numbers, however (or where entries will be linked to specific locations in the text for electronic formats), earlier iterations of the final or near-final manuscript can often be used to get a head start. Authors who are not preparing their own indexes may compile a list of important terms and preferred wordings for the indexer, but doing much more is likely to cause duplication or backtracking.

15.110 **Schedule for indexing.** Anyone making an index for the first time should know that the task is intensive and time-consuming. An index for a three-hundred-page book could take as much as three weeks' work or more. See also 15.4.

15.111 **Indexing from page proofs.** For a printed work, the indexer must have in hand a clean and complete set of proofs (usually showing final pagination) before beginning to index. A PDF version is generally more helpful than a printout because it can be used to search for specific terms (and can be printed out as needed; see also 15.114). For a journal volume, the work may begin when the first issue to be indexed has been paginated, and it may continue for several months, until page proofs for the final issue in the volume have been generated. For electronic formats, where index entries are linked to their location in the text, additional considerations may apply (see 15.13). See also 15.109, 15.116–24.

15.112 **Publisher's indexing preferences.** Before beginning work, the indexer should know the publisher's preferences in such matters as alphabetizing, run-in or indented style, inclusive numbers, handling of numeric headings, and the like (all matters dealt with in earlier sections of this chapter). For a journal volume index, the style is likely to be well established, and the indexer must follow that style. If the publisher requests an index of a particular length, the indexer should adjust the normal editing time accordingly. See also 15.130.

15.113 **Indexing tools.** The dedicated indexing programs used by many professional indexers automate such tasks as cross-referencing and the collation of entries and subentries and include special options for alphabetizing—for example, to exclude certain words or characters and to conform to either the letter-by-letter or word-by-word system (see 15.66). Such programs, however, tend to require more learning time than most authors can afford (see 15.4). Fortunately, an index can be prepared according to the guidelines in this chapter by simply entering terms and locators into a separate document using an ordinary word processor—though cross-references and alphabetizing, in particular, will need to be checked manually throughout the process (see 15.65; see also 15.5). For the latest information about tools for indexing, consult the website of the American Society for Indexing.

15.114 **Using the electronic files to index.** Publishers' policies vary as to whether they can agree to supply indexers with page proofs in electronic form. A searchable PDF file can be helpful in double-checking that additional instances of particular terms have not been overlooked. Some indexers may prefer also to annotate and refer to the PDF rather than a paper copy as they create the index. It should be noted, however, that an index cannot be automatically "generated" from a PDF file and that there is no substitute for rereading the whole work. See also 15.5, 15.118.

15.115 **Formatting index entries.** Consult with the publisher up front to determine whether a run-in or indented index is required (see 15.24–28) and whether there are any other specific requirements. Format the manuscript accordingly, using a flush-and-hang style (see 15.24). See also 15.130.

Marking Proofs and Preparing Entries

15.116 **Beginning to highlight and enter terms.** After a perusal of the table of contents and the work as a whole, an indexer should begin highlighting terms to be used as main headings or subheadings. This is normally done by hand-marking a set of proofs (on either paper or PDF). Inexperienced indexers are advised to mark the proofs—at least in the early stages—with the same kind of detail as is illustrated in figure 15.1. (Marking up the proofs in this way is less important for experienced indexers, who typically enter terms into their indexing software as they are encountered in the text.) Most indexers prefer to mark one section (or chapter) at a time and—using a word processor or dedicated indexing software (see 15.113)—to enter and alphabetize the marked terms in that section before going on to the next section. The notes belonging to the section, even if endnotes, should be checked and, if necessary, indexed at the same time (see 15.33). As the indexer becomes more skilled in marking the proofs, less underlining and fewer marginal notes may suffice.

those who find the hurting of others fun, no arguments against it can fully succeed, and the history of efforts to explain why "human nature" includes such impulses and what we might do to combat them could fill a library: books on the history of Satan and the Fall, on the cosmogonies of other cultures, on our genetic inheritance, including recently the structure of our brains, on sadism and why it is terrible or defensible. And so on. I'll just hope that here we can all agree that to hurt or harm for the fun of it is self-evidently not a loving choice.[1]

One embarrassing qualification: we amateurish amateurs do often inflict pain on others. We just don't do it on purpose.

Work and Play, _Work as Play_   : as play –56   : work as –56

To celebrate playing for the love of it risks downgrading the work we do that we love. In fact we amateurs are often tempted to talk snobbishly about those who cannot claim that what they do they do for the love of it. As Bliss Perry put the danger: "[T]he prejudice which the amateur feels toward the professional, the more or less veiled hostility between the man who does something for love which another man does for money, is one of those instinctive reactions—like the vague alarm of some wild creature in the woods—which give a hint of danger."   : loving one's

     : of one's work

The words "professional" and "work" are almost as ambiguous as the word "love." Some work is fun, some gruesome. Churchill loved his work—but needed to escape it regularly. I hated most of the farm work I did as an adolescent, and escaped it as soon as possible. I hated having to dig ditches eight hours a day for twenty-five cents an hour. Yet working as a teacher and a scholar, I have loved most of my duties—even the drudgery parts. A member of the Chicago Symphony Orchestra told me that he hates his work—his playing—and is eager for retirement. Politicians celebrate work as what will save welfare recipients from degradation; for them, to require people to work, even if they're underpaid and even if the job is awful, is a virtuous act.   : work celebrated by

Winston

Johan   Such a mishmash of implied definitions makes it impossible to place work in any simple opposition to play or pleasure. In _Homo Ludens_ Huizinga occasionally writes as if the whole point of life were to have fun by _escaping_   54 – 55

Walter

1. A fine discussion of the dangers threatened by "doing things for the love of the doing" is given by Roger Shattuck in _Forbidden Knowledge_. Shattuck argues that the art-for-art's-sake movement, with its many echoes of Pater's celebration of "burning" with a "hard, gemlike flame" and living for the "highest quality" of a given moment, risks moving us toward "worship of pure experience without restraint of any kind." The temptations of sadistic ecstasies lurk in the wings. As I shall insist again and again, to make sense out of a title like _For the Love of It_ requires careful distinction among diverse "loves," many of them potentially harmful.

FIGURE 15.1. Sample page of proof from Wayne Booth's _For the Love of It_, marked up for indexing. See 15.116–24.

15.117 **Deciding how many terms to mark.** The number of terms to mark on any one page obviously depends on the kind of work being indexed. As a very rough guide, an average of five references per text page in a book will yield a modest index (one-fiftieth the length of the text), whereas fifteen or more will yield a fairly long index (about one-twentieth the length of the text or more). If the publisher has budgeted for a strictly limited number of pages, the indexer should work accordingly. Remember that it is always easier to drop entries than to add them; err on the side of inclusiveness. See also 15.30, 15.31, 15.32–39, 15.112.

15.118 **How to mark index entries.** To visualize the method advocated here, suppose you are indexing a chapter from Wayne Booth's *For the Love of It* (University of Chicago Press, 1999), a consideration of work and play and work as play (see fig. 15.1). You have read through the chapter once and now have to go back and select headings and subheadings for indexing this particular section (of which only the first paragraphs are shown here). You decide that the whole section (pp. 54–56) will have to be indexed under both *work* and *play*, so you mark the section head as shown. (On the marked proofs, a colon separates a proposed principal heading from a proposed subheading.) Going down the page, you underline *Bliss Perry* (which will of course be inverted—Perry, Bliss—as a heading; similarly for the other personal names). You also underline *amateur* and *professional* (modifying them to the plural). In the second paragraph, you underline *work* and *love*, with proposed subheads, and *Churchill* (noting the first name in the margin). You decide to index *Chicago Symphony Orchestra*—which in another work might be tangential but here ties in with the book's major subtheme of musical performance and appreciation—and also mark *politicians*, with proposed subhead. You underline *Huizinga* (adding "Johan" in the margin) and the work *Homo Ludens*, which might also be a subheading under "Huizinga, Johan." Because the sentence spans two pages, you write "54–55" in the right margin. In the note, you mark two names (supplying a first name for Pater), one title, and one additional term (see also 15.33).

15.119 **Planning index subentries.** For each term marked, you should make an effort to write in a modification—a word or phrase that narrows the application of the heading, hence a potential subentry. Although some such modifications may eventually be dropped, they should be kept on hand in case they are needed. Otherwise you may end up with some headings that are followed by nothing but a long string of numbers, which makes for an all but useless index entry. The modifications can be altered and added to as the indexing proceeds.

15.120 **Recording inclusive numbers for index terms.** If a text discussion extends over more than one page, section, or paragraph, both beginning and ending numbers—which will depend on what locator system is being used (see 15.12)—must be recorded. See also 15.14.

15.121 **Typing and modifying index entries.** Most entries at this stage will include three elements: a heading, a modification (or provisional subentry), and a locator (page or paragraph number). While typing, you will probably modify some of the headings and add, delete, or alter subheadings and locators (a process that may at the same time entail changes to cross-references and to alphabetical order). After typing each entry, read it carefully against the page proofs—in particular, checking that the page numbers or other locators are correct. You are unlikely to have time to read your final index manuscript against the marked-up proofs, though you should certainly retain the proofs for reference until the work has been published. See also 15.115.

15.122 **Alphabetizing entries as part of the indexing process.** Many indexers alphabetize as they type; others let their software do it, intervening as necessary. By this time the indexer should have decided whether to use the letter-by-letter or the word-by-word system (see 15.66–69). If the system chosen proves unsatisfactory for the particular work as the index proceeds, a switch can be made if the publisher agrees. See also 15.65.

15.123 **Final check of indexed proofs.** After typing all the entries, read quickly through the marked-up proofs once again to see whether anything indexable has been omitted. You may find some unmarked items that seemed peripheral at the time but now, in the light of themes developed in later chapters, declare themselves to be significant. Or you may have missed major items. Now is the time to remedy all omissions.

15.124 **Noting errors during indexing.** Although not engaged to proofread, the indexer has to read carefully and usually finds a number of typographical errors and minor inconsistencies. If indexing a book (rather than a journal volume, most of which will already have been published), keep track of all such errors and send a list to the publisher (who will be very grateful) when, or before, submitting the index.

Editing and Refining the Entries

15.125 **Refining the terms for main headings.** The assembled entries must now be edited to a coherent whole. You have to make a final choice among synonymous or closely related terms—*agriculture, farming,* or *crop raising; clothing, costume,* or *dress; life, existence,* or *being*—and, if you think necessary, prepare suitable cross-references to reflect those choices. It is possible that you have already made many of these editing decisions as you entered terms into the index, in which case editing the index will also involve finalizing and checking those decisions. For journals, the terms may have been established in the indexes for previous volumes and should be retained.

15.126 **Main entries versus subentries.** You also have to decide whether certain items are best treated as main entries or as subentries under another heading. Where will readers look first? In a work dealing with schools of various kinds, such terms as *kindergarten, elementary school, middle school,* and *public school* should constitute separate entries; in a work in which those terms appear but are not the primary subject matter, they may be better treated as subentries under *school.* An index with relatively few main entries but masses of subentries is unhelpful as a search tool. Furthermore, in an indented index an excessively long string of subentries may begin to look like a set of main entries, so that users lose their way alphabetically. Promote subentries to main entries and use the alphabet to its best advantage.

15.127 **When to furnish subentries.** Main headings unmodified by subentries should not be followed by more than five or six locators. If, for example, the draft index of a work on health care includes an entry like the first example below, it should be broken up into a number of subentries, such as those in the second example, to lead readers quickly to the information sought. The extra space needed is a small price to pay for their convenience.

hospitals, 17, 22, 23, 24, 25, 28, 29–31, 33, 35, 36, 38, 42, 91–92, 94, 95, 96, 98, 101, 111–14, 197

becomes

hospitals: administration of, 22, 96; and demand for patient services, 23, 91–92; efficiency of, 17, 29–31, 33, 111–14; finances of, 28, 33, 36, 38, 42, 95, 112; and length of patient stay, 35, 94, 98, 101, 197; quality control in, 22–25, 31

15.128 **How to phrase subheadings.** Subheadings should be as concise and informative as possible and begin with a keyword likely to be sought. *A, an,* and *the* are omitted whenever possible. Example A below, *not* to be emulated, shows poorly worded and rambling subheadings. Example B shows greatly improved subentries that conserve space. Note the page references immediately following the main entry; when a main entry has one or more subentries, such undifferentiated locators should normally be reserved for definitive or extended discussions of the term (some indexers will prefer to add *defined* or a similar subhead). Example C adds sub-subentries, making for quicker reference but requiring more space (see 15.27, 15.28). For arrangement of subentries, see 15.76–78.

Example A (*not* to be emulated)

house renovation
  balancing heating system, 65
  building permit required, 7
  called "rehabbing," 8
  correcting overloaded electrical
    circuits, 136
  how wallboard is finished, 140–44
  installing ready-made fireplace,
    191–205
  painting outside of house adds
    value, 11
  plumbing permit required, 7
  removing paint from doors and
    woodwork, 156–58

  repairing dripping faucets, 99–100
  replacing clogged water pipes,
    125–28
  replacing old wiring, 129–34
  separate chimney required for
    fireplace, 192
  straightening sagging joists, 40–42
  termite damage to sills a problem,
    25
  three ways to deal with broken
    plaster, 160–62
  violations of electrical code corrected, 135
  what is involved in, 5

Example B (improvement with fairly inclusive subentries)

house renovation, 5, 8
  electrical repairs, 129–34, 135, 136
  fireplace, installing, 191–205
  heating system, balancing, 65
  legal requirements, 7, 135, 192

  painting and decorating, 11, 156–58
  plaster repair, 160–62
  plumbing repairs, 99–100, 125–28
  structural problems, 25, 40–42
  wallboard, finishing, 140–44

Example C (improvement with sub-subentries)

house renovation, 5, 8
  electrical repairs: circuit overload,
    136; code violations, 135; old
    wiring, 129–34
  heating system: balancing, 65;
    fireplace installation, 191–205
  legal requirements: electrical
    code, 135; permits, 7; separate
    chimney for fireplace, 192
  painting and decorating: painting

    exterior, 11; stripping wood-
    work, 156–58
  plumbing repairs: clogged water
    pipes, 125–28; dripping faucets,
    99–100
  structural problems: sagging joists,
    40–42; termite damage, 25
  wall and ceiling repairs: broken
    plaster, 160–62; wallboard,
    finishing, 140–44

If it looks as though an index is going to require a great many sub-subentries, the indexer should check with the publisher before proceeding.

15.129   **Checking cross-references against edited index headings.** As a final or near-final step in editing the index, make sure that all cross-references match the edited headings. And if two entries are double-posted (see 15.16), make sure they have identical locators. The following examples need their locators made consistent.

FBI (Federal Bureau of Investigation),   Churchill, Winston
      26, 98–99   on Curzon Line, 45–46, 50, 100
Federal Bureau of Investigation (FBI),   Curzon Line
      98–99 [*add* 26 (or delete 26 from   Churchill on, 45–46, 100 [*add* 50
      above)]   (or delete 50 from above)]

See also 15.15–23.

Submitting the Index

15.130   **Index submission format.** Having carefully proofread the draft and checked alphabetical order and all cross-references, punctuation, and capitalization to ensure consistency—and having produced an index of the required length, if one has been specified—you will now send the final draft to the publisher. If the publisher requires a printout, allow margins of at least one inch both left and right, and leave the text unjustified. Do not format the index in columns. Use hard returns only at the end of each entry and, for an indented-style index (see 15.26), at the end of each subentry. Use single line spacing, and apply hanging indents using your software's indentation feature (see 15.24; see also 2.14). Do not impose end-of-line hyphenation (see 2.16). If there is more than one index, give each an appropriate title (Author Index, Subject Index, etc.) and save each in a separate file. To avert disaster, keep a copy of the final draft that you send to the publisher, as well as your marked-up proofs, until the work has been published. Send the publisher a list of any errors you have found (see 15.124).

EDITING AN INDEX FOR PUBLICATION

15.131   **Evaluating an index.** Editing a well-prepared index, whether it has been created by a professional indexer or by the author, can be a pleasure.

Little work should be needed to get it ready for publication. A poorly prepared one, however, presents serious problems. As an editor, you cannot remake a really bad index. If an index cannot be repaired, you have two choices: Omit it or have a new one made by another indexer (at additional cost).

15.132 **Index-editing checklist.** Editing an index requires some or all of the following steps, not necessarily in the order given here. Note that it is not necessary to check every heading and every locator against the work—which would take forever—but it is necessary to read the index carefully and to refer to the latest version of the page proofs from time to time.

1. Check headings—in both the main entries and subentries—for alphabetical order.
2. Check the spelling, capitalization, and font (i.e., italics or roman) of each heading, consulting the page proofs if in doubt.
3. Check punctuation—commas, colons, semicolons, en dashes, etc.—for proper style and consistency (see 15.102–8).
4. Check cross-references to make sure they go somewhere and that headings match (see 15.21). Make sure they are needed; if only a few locators are involved, substitute these for the *see* reference (see 15.16). Ensure that the placement of all cross-references within entries is consistent.
5. Add cross-references you believe are necessary.
6. Check to make sure there are no false locators such as "193–93" or "12102" (and figure out whether these may be the product of a typo) and make sure the locators to each main heading and subheading are in ascending order.
7. Check subentries for consistency of order, whether alphabetical or chronological. See 15.76–78.
8. If some entries seem overanalyzed (many subentries with only one locator or, worse, with the same locator), try to combine some of them if it can be done without sacrificing their usefulness. If subheadings are more elaborately worded than necessary, try to simplify them.
9. If awkward or unnecessary sub-subentries appear, correct them by adding appropriate repeated subentries or by adjusting punctuation (see 15.27, 15.28).
10. Look for long strings of unanalyzed locators and break them up, if possible, with subentries (see 15.10, 15.128).
11. Evaluate the accuracy of locators by a random check of five to ten entries. If more than one error shows up, consult the author or the indexer; every locator may have to be rechecked.
12. If the index needs trimming, delete any entries (and cross-references thereto) that you know from your work on the book are trivial, such as references to persons or places used only as examples of something. But be

careful. You may offend someone or let yourself in for a lot of work. A handful of unnecessary entries, if they are very short, will not mar an otherwise good index. It may also make sense to eliminate some subentries (expanding the number of locators allowed without modifications; see also 15.127) rather than deleting access points. Finally, in some cases it may make sense to convert an indented index to run-in format.

15.133　**Instructions for typesetting the index.** At this stage the publisher will have prepared specifications for typesetting the index, and few further instructions are needed. To avoid problems, a brief note such as the following (for an indented index to a book) may be prefixed to the index manuscript after consulting the detailed specifications:

> Set two columns, flush and hang, ragged right; indent subentries one em; indent runovers two ems; preserve en dashes between continuing numbers; leave one line space between alphabetical blocks. Set headnote across both columns. See publisher's design specifications for size and measure.

For an example of a headnote, see 15.140.

TYPOGRAPHICAL CONSIDERATIONS FOR INDEXES

15.134　**Type size and column width for indexes.** In print works, indexes are usually set in smaller type than the body of the work, often two sizes smaller. That is, if the body copy is set in ten-on-twelve-point type, and the extracts, bibliography, and appendixes in nine-on-eleven, the index will probably be set in eight-on-ten (with a blank line before each new alphabetic grouping). Indexes are usually set in two columns; with a line length of twenty-six picas (in a book with a trim size of six by nine inches), the index columns will each be twelve and a half picas wide, with a one-pica space between them. In large-format print works, however, the index may be set in three or more columns.

15.135　**Ragged right-hand margin for indexes.** For very short lines, such as those in an index, justifying the text usually results in either gaping word spaces or excessive hyphenation, making for difficult reading. Chicago therefore sets all indexes without justification ("ragged right").

15.136　**Indenting index entries.** All runover lines are indented, whether the subentries are run in or indented. In indexes with indented subentries (see 15.26), runover lines have to be indented more deeply than the subentries; all runovers, whether from a main entry or a subentry (or even a sub-subentry, should these too be indented), should be indented equally from the left margin. Thus, in an indented index the subentries may be indented one em, the sub-subentries two ems, and the runovers for all entries three ems. (For avoiding sub-subentries, see 15.27, 15.28.) All these matters, however, must be determined before type is set.

15.137 **Fixing bad breaks in indexes.** The final, typeset index should be checked for bad breaks. A line consisting of only one or two page numbers should not be left at the top of a column, for example. A single line at the end of an alphabetic section (followed by a blank line) should not head a column, nor should a single line at the beginning of an alphabetic section remain at the foot of a column. Blemishes like these are eliminated by rebreaking entries or transposing lines from one column to another, by adding to the white space between alphabetic sections, and sometimes by lengthening or shortening all columns on facing pages by one line.

15.138 **Adding "continued" lines in an index.** If an entry breaks at the foot of the last column on a right-hand page (a recto) and resumes at the top of the following left-hand page (a verso), the main heading should be repeated, followed by the word *continued* in parentheses, above the carried-over part of the index. (In an especially long or complex index it may make sense to add *continued* lines for every entry that breaks at the end of a column, as in the print edition of this manual.)

> ingestive behavior (*continued*)
>> network of causes underlying, 68;
>>> physiology of, 69–70, 86–87; in
>>>> rat, 100; in starfish, 45, 52–62

In an indented index with indented sub-subentries, it may be necessary to repeat a subentry if the subentry has been broken.

> house renovation (*continued*)
>> structural problems (*continued*)
>>> termite damage, 25–27
>>> warped overhangs, 46–49

15.139 **Making typographic distinctions in index entries.** A complicated index can sometimes be made easier to read by using different type styles or fonts. If, for example, names of writers need to be distinguished from names of literary characters, one or the other might be set in caps and small caps. Page references to illustrations might be in italic type (see

15.39) and references to the principal treatment of a subject in boldface. If devices of this kind are used, a headnote to the index must furnish a key (see 15.140, 15.142).

EXAMPLES OF INDEXES

15.140 **A run-in index with italicized references to figures and tables.** Run-in indexes are the most economical of the five formats exemplified in this section. Note the italic page references and the headnote explaining their use. Boldface could also be used for that purpose (see 15.142). For more examples and further discussion, see 15.25, 15.27, 15.102–8. See also 15.76, 15.139.

Page numbers in italics refer to figures and tables.

Abbot, George, 241–42

ABC, printing of, 164

abridgment: cases of, 246n161; as offense, 455–56, 607; of *Philosophical Transactions*, 579n83; restrictions on, 226, 227; works as, *302–3*, *316*, *316–17*

Abridgment (Croke), *302–3*

Abridgment (Rolle), *316*, *316–17*

absolutism: absence of in England, 48; arbitrary government and, 251–52, 252n182; Cromwell and, 273–74; Hobbes and, 308; patronage and, 24; property and, 253, 255; royal authorship of laws and, 312, 317, 336n29; royal prerogative and, 251, 253–54

Académie royale des sciences (France), 436, 491n91, 510, 554

If occasional sub-subentries are required in a run-in index, you may resort to the style illustrated in 15.27, example B, using em dashes.

15.141 **An indented index with run-in sub-subentries.** For further examples and discussion, see 15.28. See also 15.76.

American black bear
  compared with giant panda:
    activity, 216–17; habitat, 211–12;
    home range, 219; litter size, 221;
    movement patterns of males,
    124–26, 219
  delayed implantation in, 191
  reproductive flexibility of, 221
  See also bears
amino acid content of bamboo, 75–

76, 86, 89; compared with other
  foods, 77
artificial insemination, 179
Ascaris schroederi, 162
Asiatic black bear
  constructing sleeping nests, 140
  giant panda serologically close
    to, 228
  See also bears

15.142 **An indented index with indented sub-subentries and highlighted definitions.** Note the deep indentation for runover lines (see 15.136). A boldface page number indicates that the term is defined on that page (explained in a headnote at the beginning of the index). Italics could also be used for that purpose (see 15.140). For further discussion and examples, see 15.28. See also 15.76, 15.139.

Page numbers for definitions are in boldface.

B stars, **3**, 7, 26–27, 647
bright rims, **7**, 16, 27–28. *See also*
    nebular forms
brightness temperatures, 388, 582,
    589, 602
bulbs (in nebulae). *See* nebular forms
cameras, electronic, 492, 499
carbon flash, 559
Cassiopeia A (3C461). *See* radio
    sources; supernovae
catalogs
  of bright nebulae, 74
  of dark nebulae, 74, 120
    Lundmark, 121

Lynds, 123
  Schoenberg, 123
Herschel's (of nebulae), 119
  of planetary nebulae, 484–85, 563
    Perek-Kohoutek, 484, 563
    Vorontsov-Velyaminov, 484
  of reflection nebulae, 74
  3C catalog of radio sources, re-
    vised, 630
central stars. *See* planetary nebulae
Cerenkov radiation, **668**, 709
chemical composition, 71. *See also*
    abundances; *and names of*
    individual elements

If occasional sub-sub-subentries are essential (they should be avoided if at all possible), they must be run in to the sub-subentries in the same way as sub-subentries are run in at 15.28, example A.

15.143 **An index of first lines.** Unless all the poems, hymns, or songs indexed have very short lines, indexes of this kind are often set full measure (rather than in multiple columns) for easier reading. Note that lines beginning with *A*, *An*, or *The* are alphabetized under *A* or *T* (and are arranged below according to the word-by-word system; see 15.66).

A handful of red sand, from the hot clime, 108
After so long an absence, 295
An old man in a lodge within a park, 315
Beautiful valley! through whose verdant meads, 325
From this high portal, where upsprings, 630
O hemlock tree! O hemlock tree! how faithful are thy branches, 614
O'er all the hill-tops, 617
Of Prometheus, how undaunted, 185

The young Endymion sleeps Endymion's sleep, 316
There is no flock, however watched and tended, 107

15.144 **An index with authors, titles, and first lines combined.** To distinguish the elements, authors' names may be set in caps and small caps, titles of poems in italics, and first lines in roman type, sentence case, without quotation marks. If needed, a headnote to this effect could be furnished.

Cermak, it was, who entertained so great astonishment, 819
Certain she was that tigers fathered him, 724
CHESTERVILLE, NORA M., 212
Come, you whose loves are dead, 394
Coming Homeward Out of Spain, 73
Commemorate me before you leave me, Charlotte, 292
Complaint of a Lover Rebuked, 29
COMPTON, WILBER C., 96
Confound you, Marilyn, confound you, 459

In a general index, poem titles would be set in roman and enclosed in quotation marks, as in text or notes (see 8.183, 8.184).

Index

References are to paragraph numbers except where specified as figure (fig.).

taxonomic indexes, 15.6
technical writing. *See* scientific, technical, and medical (STM) works, indexes for
technology. *See* computer software; scientific, technical, and medical (STM) works, indexes for
territories. *See* geographic terminology
text citations, 15.37–38. *See also* authors' names
text figures. *See* illustrations
Thai names, 15.93
the, 15.56–57, 15.96, 15.99, 15.143. *See also* articles (definite and indefinite)
title case. *See* capitalization
titled persons, 15.46
titles and offices of people
    academic titles, 15.48
    nobility, 15.46
    religious titles, 15.47
    saints, 15.50
    sovereigns and other rulers, 15.45, 15.74, 15.106
    the with (*see* honorifics)
titles of works
    alphabetizing, 15.56–61, 15.64
    artworks and exhibitions, 15.58
    initial articles in, 15.56–57, 15.59–60, 15.64
    journals, 15.57
    musical works, 15.58
    newspapers and news sites, 15.56
    non-English materials (*see under* non-English materials)
    punctuation in: commas, 15.56–57; exclamation points, 15.62; question marks, 15.62
    See also bibliographies; indexing: titles of works; reference lists
topographical divisions, 15.98
transliteration and transliterated text. *See* Arabic names; Chinese names; Japanese names; Korean names; South Asian names

type size, 15.134
type styles. *See* boldface, uses of; italics, uses of; roman (type)
typesetters and typesetting, 15.133, 15.143
typographic considerations, 15.134. *See also* boldface, uses of; italics, uses of; special characters

under, in cross-references, 15.19–20
units of measurement. *See* numbers
unjustified text, 15.130, 15.135
URLs (uniform resource locators). *See* electronic publications; hyperlinks

verso pages, 15.138. *See also* page numbers (folios)
Vietnamese names, 15.94

Wade-Giles romanization system, 15.85
web-based publications. *See* electronic publications
websites and web pages. *See* electronic publications; hyperlinks
word order. *See* inverted word order; syntax
word processors, 15.5, 15.65, 15.113, 15.116, 15.130. *See also* manuscript editing, and indexes
word-by-word alphabetization
    and computerized sorting, 15.65
    for indexes of first lines, 15.143
    vs. letter-by-letter, 15.66, 15.69
    overview of, 15.68
    preferred, 15.65–66
    and word-processors' sort functions, 15.65
words, introductory, 15.76
works, entries using, 15.58
works cited lists, 15.32, 15.37–38

years. *See* dates, alphabetizing

Printed and bound by CPI Group (UK) Ltd, Croydon, CR0 4YY

20/10/2024